Copyright © 2024

All rights reserved. No part of this publication may be reproduced, modified or altered, distributed, or transmitted in any form or by any means, including photocopying, recording, or other electronic or mechanical methods, without the prior written permission of the publisher as per copyright law.

- For NIV (New International Version):

Scripture quotations are taken from the Holy Bible, New International Version®, NIV®. Copyright ©1973, 1978, 1984, 2011 by Biblica, Inc.® Used by permission of Zondervan. All rights reserved worldwide.

- For ESV (English Standard Version):

Scripture quotations are from the ESV® Bible (The Holy Bible, English Standard Version®), copyright ©2001 by Crossway, a publishing ministry of Good News Publishers. Used by permission. All rights reserved.

- For KJV (King James Version):

Scripture quotations are from the King James Version of the Bible, which is in the public domain.

- For NKJV (New King James Version):

Scripture taken from the New King James Version®. Copyright ©1982 by Thomas Nelson. Used by permission. All rights reserved.

Contact:
Greatnessvalleylifestyle.com
Greatnessvalley.com
ISBN: 978-1-7326972-9-4

"An upbeat attitude increases your happiness and productivity."

Look back at all the positive strategies you learned in the course titled "Rising Strong: Healing from Emotional Trauma, Breakups, and Betrayal or the Grief Course.

Dear Friends and Colleagues,

This journal is a safe space for you to process, reflect, and renew. May each page offer comfort, strength, and guidance as you navigate the challenges of caring for others.

You give so much; remember to hold space for your own healing, too. Let this be a journey toward resilience, balance, and peace.

With gratitude for all you do,

Diana

Table of Contents

Encouraging Bible Verses..V

Tips/Ideas for Using this Journal...VI

Compassion Fatigue..1

Self-Care and Resilience-Building 7

Creating a Self-Care Plan...13

Peer Support and Compassion Resilience...16

Safe Spaces for Emotional Expression...22

Emotion Regulation Techniques...31

Strategies for Recognizing and Validating Emotions...................................37

Healthy Expression and Release Practices...40

Multicultural Grief and Understanding..46

Balancing Professionalism and Emotional Health......................................52

Boundaries and Self-Advocacy...58

Emotional Role-Playing and Scenario Practice...70

Sustainable Coping Mechanisms...76

Self-Care Strategies List...82, 83, 84

Checking-in..87

Praying for...103

©Greatness Valley Lifestyle: *Beyond the Frontline*-Diana Rowe

Here are some encouraging Bible verses that serve as a reminder of God's presence, strength, and guidance through difficult times and daily life.

Isaiah 40:31
"But those who hope in the Lord will renew their strength. They will soar on wings like eagles; they will run and not grow weary, they will walk and not be faint."

Psalm 46:1
"God is our refuge and strength, an ever-present help in trouble."

Matthew 11:28
"Come to me, all you who are weary and burdened, and I will give you rest."

Galatians 6:9
"Let us not become weary in doing good, for at the proper time we will reap a harvest if we do not give up."

Psalm 23:4
"Even though I walk through the darkest valley, I will fear no evil, for You are with me; Your rod and Your staff, they comfort me."

Philippians 4:13
"I can do all this through Christ who gives me strength."

Psalm 73:26
"My flesh and my heart may fail, but God is the strength of my heart and my portion forever."

Isaiah 41:10
"So do not fear, for I am with you; do not be dismayed, for I am your God. I will strengthen you and help you; I will uphold you with my righteous right hand."

2 Corinthians 1:3-4
"Praise be to the God and Father of our Lord Jesus Christ, the Father of compassion and the God of all comfort, who comforts us in all our troubles so that we can comfort those in any trouble with the comfort we ourselves receive from God."

Proverbs 3:5-6
"Trust in the Lord with all your heart and lean not on your own understanding; in all your ways acknowledge Him, and He will direct your paths."

Tips/Ideas for Using this Journal

- After responding to each prompt, you can use the self-care strategy lists on pages 82-84 to determine what you need, what could help you or someone else, or what choice you can implement in the future for the desired outcome.

- There are six self-care categories to make it easy for you to understand or give you ideas about what you might need to do. You may need one or a combination of more than one from different categories to fit your individual needs.

  1. Emotional Self-Care
  2. Mental Self-Care
  3. Physical Self-Care
  4. Spiritual Self-Care
  5. Social Self-Care
  6. Professional Self-Care

  See pages 82-84

- The "self-care" lists on pages 82-84 provide great ideas for you to create your self-care plan.

- Ideas for the "check-in" section: you can use this to start your day or take a break to connect/check in on yourself, a colleague, or someone else in person or on the phone. You can also use it at the end of your day to check on yourself and make notes of your progress throughout the day.

- The Bible verses can be used as affirmations and positive encouragement throughout the day to remind you that you are seen and loved by God no matter who you are or what you're going through.

- Ideas for the "praying for" section: you can write some challenges, habits you want to break, goals, aspirations, and names of people you want to pray for on your team or those you serve.

Additional affirmations can be found at greatnessvalleylifestyle.com in the journal titled: "Empowering Beliefs."

I hope these ideas/tips will help you on your journey. Praying for your success,
Diana

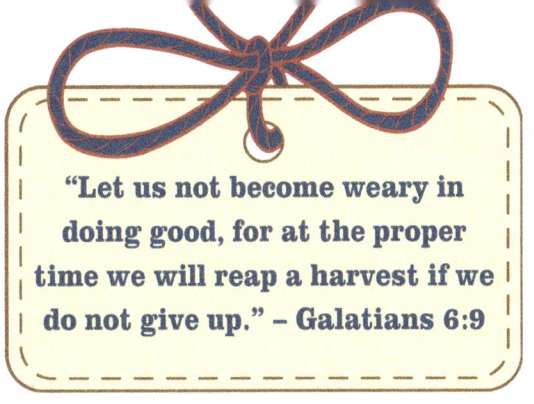

"Let us not become weary in doing good, for at the proper time we will reap a harvest if we do not give up." – Galatians 6:9

Compassion Fatigue

Write about the last time you felt emotionally drained or disconnected at work. What triggered those feelings?
- How did your body react to the stress (e.g., headaches, fatigue, irritability)?

_____
_____
_____
_____
_____
_____
_____
_____
_____
_____
_____
_____
_____

Notes

> "Let us not become weary in doing good, for at the proper time we will reap a harvest if we do not give up." – Galatians 6:9

Notes

"Let us not become weary in doing good, for at the proper time we will reap a harvest if we do not give up." – Galatians 6:9

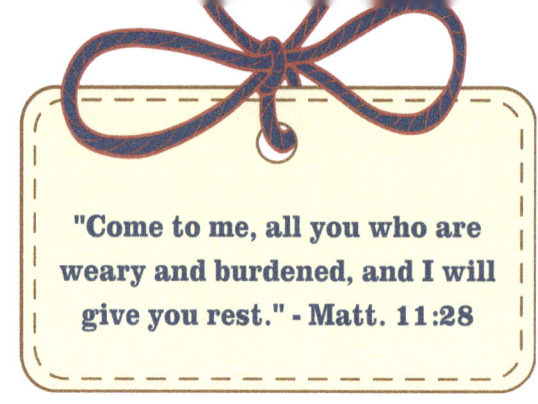

"Come to me, all you who are weary and burdened, and I will give you rest." - Matt. 11:28

Compassion Fatigue

Reflect on a time when you felt emotionally exhausted from helping a patient/client or family through a difficult situation. How did it affect your ability to continue offering compassionate care?

_____
_____
_____
_____
_____
_____
_____
_____
_____
_____
_____
_____

Notes

"Come to me, all you who are weary and burdened, and I will give you rest." - Matt. 11:28

Notes

"Come to me, all you who are weary and burdened, and I will give you rest." - Matt. 11:28

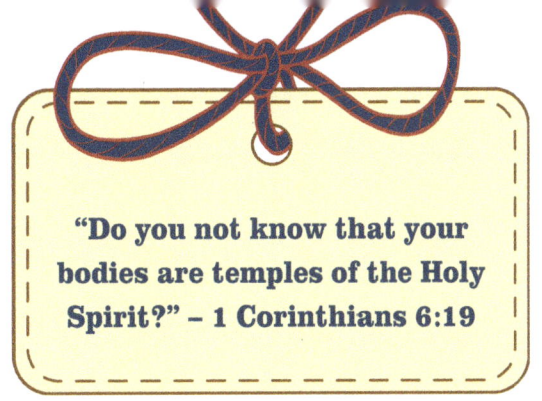
"Do you not know that your bodies are temples of the Holy Spirit?" – 1 Corinthians 6:19

Creating a Self-Care Plan

- **List three ways you currently take care of your physical health.**

Notes

"Come to me, all you who are weary and burdened, and I will give you rest." - Matt. 11:28

Notes

"Come to me, all you who are weary and burdened, and I will give you rest." - Matt. 11:28

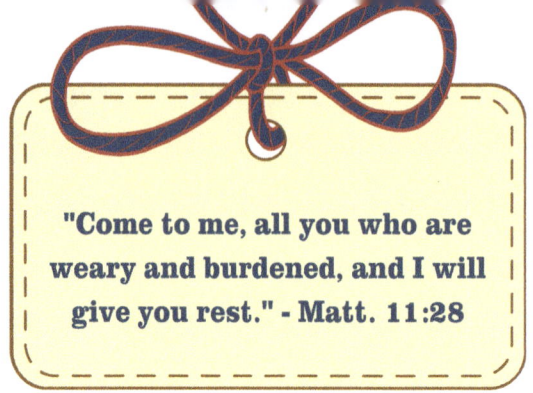

"Come to me, all you who are weary and burdened, and I will give you rest." - Matt. 11:28

Self-Care and Resilience-Building

What activities help you feel restored emotionally, mentally, and physically? Write about a time when you took a break and how it rejuvenated your spirit.

_____
_____
_____
_____
_____
_____
_____
_____
_____
_____
_____
_____

Notes

"Come to me, all you who are weary and burdened, and I will give you rest." - Matt. 11:28

Notes

"Come to me, all you who are weary and burdened, and I will give you rest." - Matt. 11:28

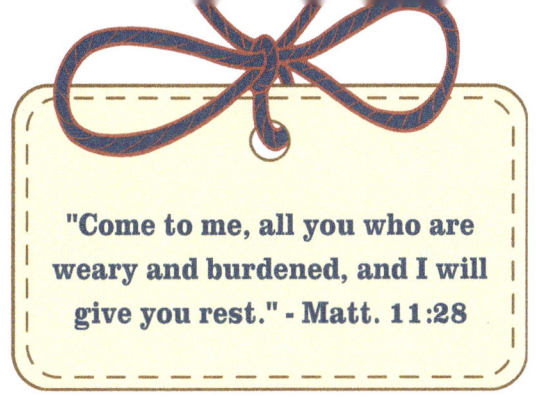

"Come to me, all you who are weary and burdened, and I will give you rest." - Matt. 11:28

Creating a Self-Care Plan

Create a weekly self-care plan. Include activities that help you feel emotionally, spiritually and physically refreshed. How will you ensure these activities become a consistent part of your routine?

_____
_____
_____
_____
_____
_____
_____
_____
_____
_____
_____
_____
_____

Notes

"Do you not know that your bodies are temples of the Holy Spirit?" – 1 Corinthians 6:19

Notes

"Come to me, all you who are weary and burdened, and I will give you rest." - Matt. 11:28

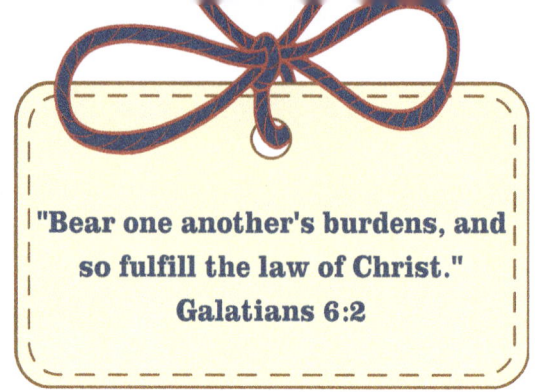

"Bear one another's burdens, and so fulfill the law of Christ."
Galatians 6:2

Peer Support and Compassion Resilience

Reflect on a time when a colleague supported you emotionally. How did that help you process your emotions and renew your sense of purpose?

_____
_____
_____
_____
_____
_____
_____
_____
_____
_____
_____
_____

ⓒGreatness Valley Lifestyle: *Beyond the Frontline*-Diana Rowe

Notes

"Bear one another's burdens, and so fulfill the law of Christ." Galatians 6:2

Notes

"Bear one another's burdens, and so fulfill the law of Christ." Galatians 6:2

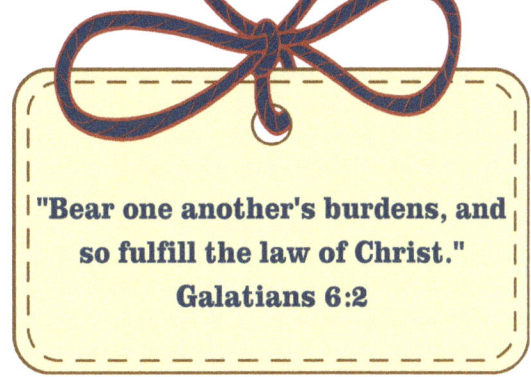

"Bear one another's burdens, and so fulfill the law of Christ."
Galatians 6:2

Peer Support and Compassion Resilience

- **Who are the people in your life that you can lean on during difficult times?**

_____
_____
_____
_____
_____
_____
_____
_____
_____
_____
_____
_____
_____
_____

Notes

> "Bear one another's burdens, and so fulfill the law of Christ."
> Galatians 6:2

Notes

"Bear one another's burdens, and so fulfill the law of Christ." Galatians 6:2

"Rejoice with those who rejoice; mourn with those who mourn." – Romans 12:15

Safe Spaces for Emotional Expression

Identify a safe space (physical or emotional) where you feel comfortable expressing your emotions. What makes this space conducive to emotional release?

_____
_____
_____
_____
_____
_____
_____
_____
_____
_____
_____
_____

Notes

> "Rejoice with those who rejoice; mourn with those who mourn." – Romans 12:15

Notes

"Rejoice with those who rejoice; mourn with those who mourn." – Romans 12:15

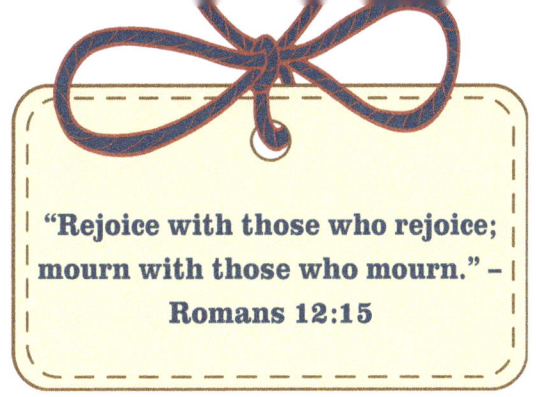

"Rejoice with those who rejoice; mourn with those who mourn." – Romans 12:15

Safe Spaces for Emotional Expression

- What fears or beliefs make it difficult for you to share your emotions with others?

Notes

"Rejoice with those who rejoice; mourn with those who mourn." – Romans 12:15

Notes

"Rejoice with those who rejoice; mourn with those who mourn." – Romans 12:15

"Rejoice with those who rejoice; mourn with those who mourn." – Romans 12:15

Safe Spaces for Emotional Expression

- **Think of a time someone trusted you with their vulnerability. How did you respond?**

_____
_____
_____
_____
_____
_____
_____
_____
_____
_____
_____
_____

Notes

> "Rejoice with those who rejoice; mourn with those who mourn." – Romans 12:15

Notes

"Rejoice with those who rejoice; mourn with those who mourn." – Romans 12:15

Emotion Regulation Techniques

- **What situations or interactions tend to trigger strong emotions for you?**

_____
_____
_____
_____
_____
_____
_____
_____
_____
_____
_____
_____

Notes

"Be quick to listen, slow to speak, and slow to become angry."
James 1:19

Notes

"Be quick to listen, slow to speak, and slow to become angry."
James 1:19

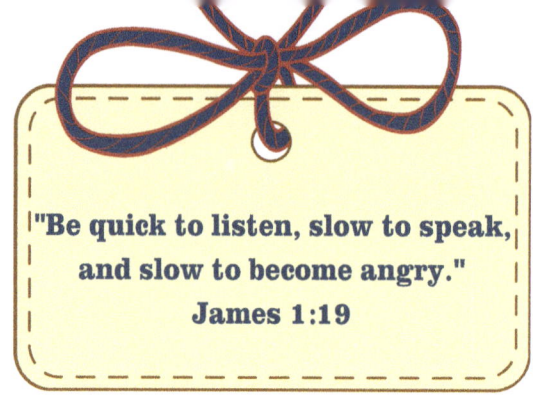

"Be quick to listen, slow to speak, and slow to become angry."
James 1:19

Emotion Regulation Techniques

Write about an emotional situation you experienced at work.
How did you manage your emotions in that moment?
What strategies helped you stay calm?

Notes

"Be quick to listen, slow to speak, and slow to become angry." James 1:19

Notes

"Be quick to listen, slow to speak, and slow to become angry."
James 1:19

"Be quick to listen, slow to speak, and slow to become angry."
James 1:19

Strategies for Recognizing and Validating Emotions

Take a moment to identify the emotions you're feeling today. Are they related to work, personal life, or both? How can you validate these emotions without judgment?

_____
_____
_____
_____
_____
_____
_____
_____
_____
_____
_____
_____
_____

Notes

> "Be quick to listen, slow to speak, and slow to become angry."
> James 1:19

Notes

"Be quick to listen, slow to speak, and slow to become angry."
James 1:19

"Pour out your heart like water in the presence of the Lord." – Lamentations 2:19

Healthy Expression and Release Practices

- What signals (e.g., irritability, tension, or withdrawal) does your body give you when you need to release pent-up emotions?

_____
_____
_____
_____
_____
_____
_____
_____
_____
_____
_____
_____

Notes

> "Pour out your heart like water in the presence of the Lord."
>
> – Lamentations 2:19

Notes

> "Pour out your heart like water in the presence of the Lord."
> – Lamentations 2:19

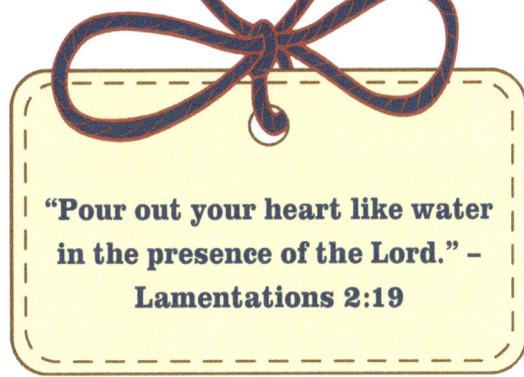

"Pour out your heart like water in the presence of the Lord." – Lamentations 2:19

Healthy Expression and Release Practices

Write about an activity that helps you express your feelings, such as journaling, prayer, singing, or exercising. How does it help you feel lighter?

_____
_____
_____
_____
_____
_____
_____
_____
_____
_____
_____
_____

Notes

> "Pour out your heart like water in the presence of the Lord."
> – Lamentations 2:19

Notes

"Pour out your heart like water in the presence of the Lord."

– Lamentations 2:19

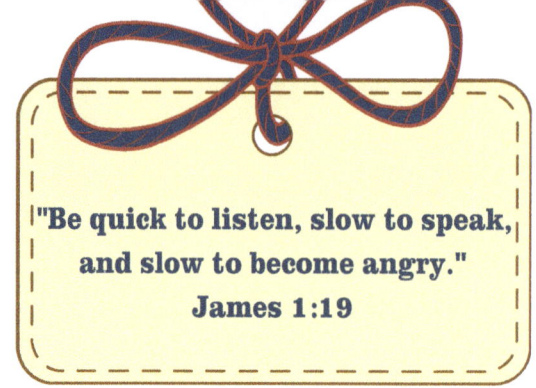

"Be quick to listen, slow to speak, and slow to become angry."
James 1:19

Multicultural Grief and Understanding

- Reflect on how your cultural background shapes the way you process grief. What traditions, beliefs, or rituals have been meaningful to you?

Notes

"Be quick to listen, slow to speak, and slow to become angry."
James 1:19

Notes

"Be quick to listen, slow to speak, and slow to become angry."
James 1:19

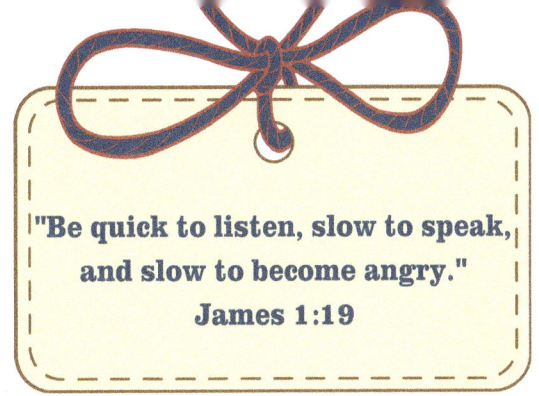

"Be quick to listen, slow to speak, and slow to become angry."
James 1:19

Multicultural Grief and Understanding

- **Reflect on your experiences working with patients, students, clients and families from different cultural backgrounds. Think of a time when someone from a different culture grieved in a way unfamiliar to you. What did you learn from their approach?**

_____
_____
_____
_____
_____
_____
_____
_____
_____
_____
_____
_____

Notes

"Be quick to listen, slow to speak, and slow to become angry."
James 1:19

Notes

"Be quick to listen, slow to speak, and slow to become angry."
James 1:19

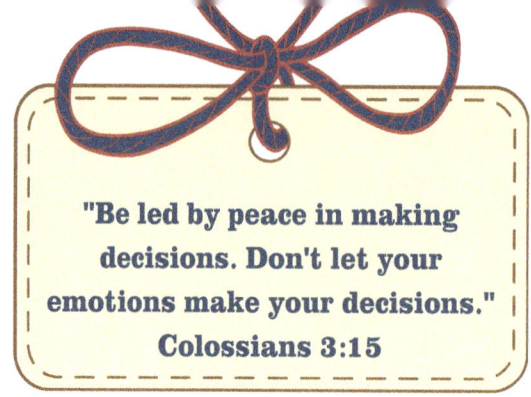

"Be led by peace in making decisions. Don't let your emotions make your decisions."
Colossians 3:15

Balancing Professionalism and Emotional Health

- Reflect on a time when personal emotions affected your ability to stay professional. What made that moment difficult?

_____
_____
_____
_____
_____
_____
_____
_____
_____
_____
_____
_____

Notes

"Be led by peace in making decisions. Don't let your emotions make your decisions." Colossians 3:15

Notes

"Be led by peace in making decisions. Don't let your emotions make your decisions."
Colossians 3:15

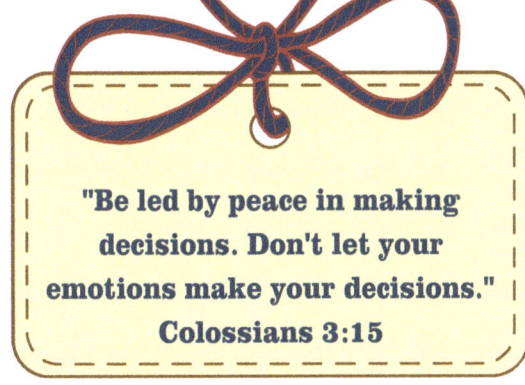

"Be led by peace in making decisions. Don't let your emotions make your decisions."
Colossians 3:15

Balancing Professionalism and Emotional Health

Describe a situation where you had to balance your emotions with professional expectations. How did you manage to maintain professionalism while also offering compassionate care?

_____
_____
_____
_____
_____
_____
_____
_____
_____
_____
_____

Notes

> "Be led by peace in making decisions. Don't let your emotions make your decisions."
> Colossians 3:15

Notes

"Be led by peace in making decisions. Don't let your emotions make your decisions." Colossians 3:15

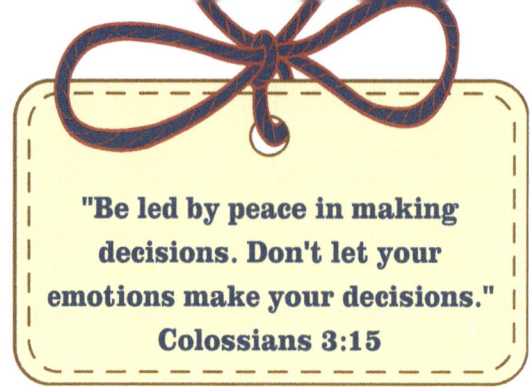

"Be led by peace in making decisions. Don't let your emotions make your decisions."
Colossians 3:15

Boundaries and Self-Advocacy

What boundaries do you need to set at work to protect your emotional well-being? How will you communicate these boundaries to your team?

_____
_____
_____
_____
_____
_____
_____
_____
_____
_____
_____
_____

Notes

"Be led by peace in making decisions. Don't let your emotions make your decisions." Colossians 3:15

Notes

"Be led by peace in making decisions. Don't let your emotions make your decisions." Colossians 3:15

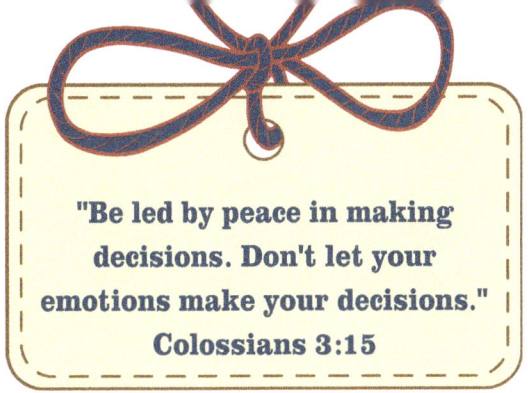

"Be led by peace in making decisions. Don't let your emotions make your decisions."
Colossians 3:15

**How do you currently set boundaries with patients, clients, students, or colleagues?
What emotions arise when you say "no" or set limits?
Reflect on a time when maintaining boundaries helped you care more effectively.**

_____
_____
_____
_____
_____
_____
_____
_____
_____
_____
_____
_____

Notes

"Be led by peace in making decisions. Don't let your emotions make your decisions." Colossians 3:15

Notes

"Be led by peace in making decisions. Don't let your emotions make your decisions." Colossians 3:15

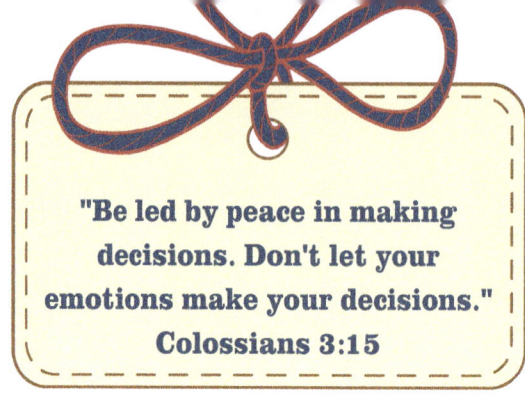

"Be led by peace in making decisions. Don't let your emotions make your decisions."
Colossians 3:15

Describe a situation where you felt overwhelmed by someone else's needs. How could boundaries have changed the outcome?

_____
_____
_____
_____
_____
_____
_____
_____
_____
_____
_____
_____
_____
_____

Notes

> "Be led by peace in making decisions. Don't let your emotions make your decisions." Colossians 3:15

Notes

"Be led by peace in making decisions. Don't let your emotions make your decisions."
Colossians 3:15

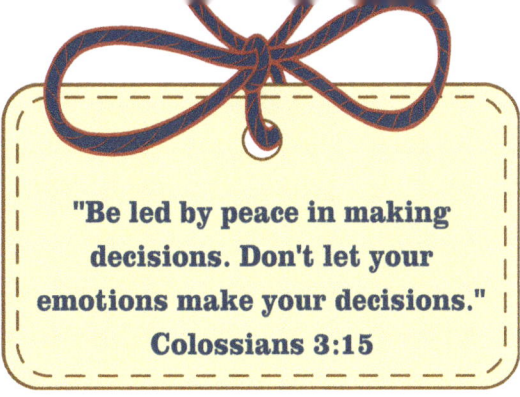

"Be led by peace in making decisions. Don't let your emotions make your decisions."
Colossians 3:15

List three ways you can honor your empathy without losing yourself in others' pain.

Notes

"Be led by peace in making decisions. Don't let your emotions make your decisions." Colossians 3:15

Notes

"Be led by peace in making decisions. Don't let your emotions make your decisions."
Colossians 3:15

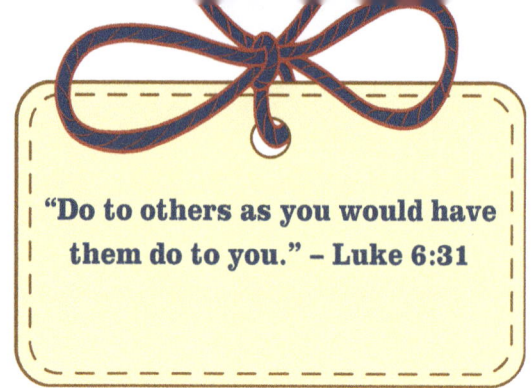

"Do to others as you would have them do to you." – Luke 6:31

Emotional Role-Playing and Scenario Practice

Think of a challenging scenario you face at work (e.g., delivering bad news, comforting a grieving family). Role-play this scenario in your journal. How do you want to respond in a way that balances professionalism and compassion?

_____
_____
_____
_____
_____
_____
_____
_____
_____
_____
_____

Notes

> "Do to others as you would have them do to you."
> – Luke 6:31

Notes

"Do to others as you would have them do to you." – Luke 6:31

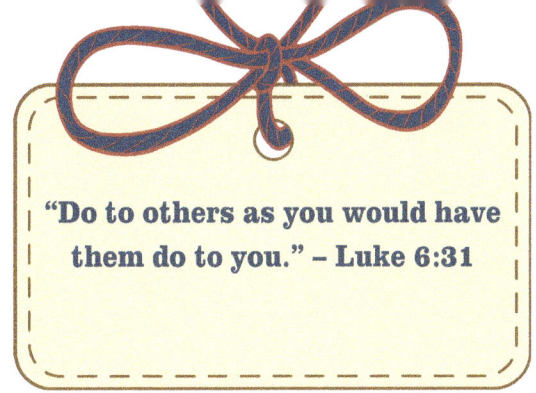

"Do to others as you would have them do to you." – Luke 6:31

Emotional Role-Playing and Scenario Practice

Practice responding to common emotional reactions like anger, tears, or withdrawal. How can you stay calm and supportive?

_____
_____
_____
_____
_____
_____
_____
_____
_____
_____
_____

Notes

> "Do to others as you would have them do to you."
> – Luke 6:31

Notes

"Do to others as you would have them do to you." – Luke 6:31

"In the multitude of my anxieties within me, Your comforts bring joy to my soul."
Psalm 94:19

Sustainable Coping Mechanisms

- **Reflect on your current ways of managing stress or grief. Are they helping you in the long run, or do they provide only temporary relief?**

_____
_____
_____
_____
_____
_____
_____
_____
_____
_____
_____

Notes

> "In the multitude of my anxieties within me, Your comforts bring joy to my soul."
> Psalm 94:19

Notes

"In the multitude of my anxieties within me, Your comforts bring joy to my soul."
Psalm 94:19

"In the multitude of my anxieties within me, Your comforts bring joy to my soul."
Psalm 94:19

Sustainable Coping Mechanisms

List five sustainable coping mechanisms that you can use in your daily routine. These could include prayer, Christian music meditation, exercise, or talking with a trusted friend. How can you incorporate these into your daily work life?

_____
_____
_____
_____
_____
_____
_____
_____
_____
_____
_____
_____

Notes

"In the multitude of my anxieties within me, Your comforts bring joy to my soul."
Psalm 94:19

Notes

"In the multitude of my anxieties within me, Your comforts bring joy to my soul."
Psalm 94:19

Self-Care Strategies List

Emotional Self-Care:

1. **Journaling:** Write about daily experiences, emotions, and reflections to process feelings.
2. **Breathing Exercises:** Use techniques like deep breathing to ground yourself and reduce anxiety.
3. **Emotional Check-Ins:** Take moments throughout the day to pause and identify what you're feeling.
4. **Limit Exposure to Stressful Media:** Take breaks from news or social media that might add to emotional stress.
5. **Express Yourself Creatively:** Engage in art, Christian music etc.

Mental Self-Care:

1. **Set Boundaries:** Establish limits for work, social media, and personal obligations to prevent overload.
2. **Engage in a Hobby:** Spend time doing something you enjoy, such as reading, crafting, or gardening.
3. **Practice Gratitude:** Keep a gratitude journal and write down three things you're thankful for each day.
4. **Stay Organized:** Use planners or apps to manage tasks and reduce mental clutter.
5. **Learn Something New:** Pick up a new skill or take an online course for mental stimulation.

Self-Care Strategies List

Physical Self-Care:

1. **Exercise Regularly:** Find enjoyable physical activities, like walking or simple workouts.
2. **Prioritize Sleep:** Aim for consistent sleep patterns to help restore and rejuvenate your body.
3. **Eat Nourishing Foods:** Focus on balanced meals with adequate hydration for sustained energy.
4. **Take Short Breaks:** Step outside for fresh air or quickly stretch during the day to re-energize.
5. **Wash your hair and take a long bath.**
6. **Omit Caffeine and Sugar:** Avoid over-reliance on stimulants that may lead to energy crashes later.

Spiritual Self-Care:

1. **Daily Prayer and Bible reading:** Start and end the day with quiet reflection, prayer, Bible lessons/verse, or meditative breathing.
2. **Read Inspirational Texts:** Find motivation and solace in positive books, scriptures, or poems that inspire you.
3. **Practice Compassion for Yourself and Others:** Cultivate kindness toward yourself and others as a daily habit.
4. **Spend Time in Nature:** Connect with the natural world to find peace and perspective.
5. **Set Intentions:** Begin each day by setting a positive intention for how you want to feel or what you want to focus on.

Self-Care Strategies List

Social Self-Care:
1. **Connect with Loved Ones:** Make time to talk or meet with family and friends who bring positivity to your life.
2. **Find a Support Group:** Join *trusted* groups or communities where you can openly share experiences and feelings.
3. **Seek Peer Support:** Reach out to *trusted* colleagues or friends who understand your work challenges.
4. **Ask for Help:** Be open to receiving help when you need it, and recognize that seeking support is a strength.
5. **Limit Time with Draining Individuals:** Protect your energy by managing interactions with people who bring you down.

Professional Self-Care:
1. **Set Work-Life Boundaries:** Keep work and personal life separate to avoid burnout.
2. **Advocate for Yourself:** Speak up about your needs for breaks or help at work when necessary.
3. **Take Professional/Personal Development Courses:** Find growth opportunities that can make your job feel more rewarding.
4. **Reflect on Accomplishments:** Acknowledge your achievements and positive contributions at work.
5. **Practice Leaving Work at Work:** Create a ritual to "end" the workday mentally, especially when working from home.

Notes

> "In the multitude of my anxieties within me, Your comforts bring joy to my soul."
> Psalm 94:19

Notes

"In the multitude of my anxieties within me, Your comforts bring joy to my soul." Psalm 94:19

Checking - in

How are you *feeling* today? _____

Things you are *grateful* for :
1. _____
2. _____
3. _____

Today's affirmations : _____
_____
_____

My mood today is...

- ○ Calm
- ○ Happy
- ○ Anxious
- ○ Rested
- ○ Angry
- ○ Playful
- ○ Creative
- ○ Sad
- ○ _____

Notes

"In the multitude of my anxieties within me, Your comforts bring joy to my soul."
Psalm 94:19

Checking - in

How are you *feeling* today? _____

Things you are *grateful* for :
1. _____
2. _____
3. _____

Today's affirmations : _____
_____
_____

My mood today is...

- ○ Calm
- ○ Rested
- ○ Creative
- ○ Happy
- ○ Angry
- ○ Sad
- ○ Anxious
- ○ Playful
- ○ _____

Notes

"In the multitude of my anxieties within me, Your comforts bring joy to my soul."
Psalm 94:19

Checking - in

How are you *feeling* today? _____

Things you are *grateful* for :
1. _____
2. _____
3. _____

Today's affirmations : _____
_____
_____

My mood today is...

- ○ Calm
- ○ Happy
- ○ Anxious

- ○ Rested
- ○ Angry
- ○ Playful

- ○ Creative
- ○ Sad
- ○ _____

Notes

"In the multitude of my anxieties within me, Your comforts bring joy to my soul."
Psalm 94:19

Checking - in

How are you *feeling* today? _____

Things you are *grateful* for :

1. _____
2. _____
3. _____

Today's affirmations : _____

My mood today is...

- ○ Calm
- ○ Happy
- ○ Anxious
- ○ Rested
- ○ Angry
- ○ Playful
- ○ Creative
- ○ Sad
- ○ _____

Notes

"In the multitude of my anxieties within me, Your comforts bring joy to my soul."
Psalm 94:19

Checking - in

How are you *feeling* today? _____

Things you are *grateful* for :
1. _____
   _____
2. _____
   _____
3. _____
   _____

Today's affirmations : _____
_____
_____

My mood today is...

- ○ Calm
- ○ Happy
- ○ Anxious

- ○ Rested
- ○ Angry
- ○ Playful

- ○ Creative
- ○ Sad
- ○ _____

Notes

"In the multitude of my anxieties within me, Your comforts bring joy to my soul."
Psalm 94:19

Checking - in

How are you *feeling* today? _____

Things you are *grateful* for :

1. _____
2. _____
3. _____

Today's affirmations : _____
_____
_____

My mood today is...

- ○ Calm
- ○ Happy
- ○ Anxious

- ○ Rested
- ○ Angry
- ○ Playful

- ○ Creative
- ○ Sad
- ○ _____

Notes

"In the multitude of my anxieties within me, Your comforts bring joy to my soul."
Psalm 94:19

Checking - in

How are you *feeling* today? _____

Things you are *grateful* for :
1. _____
2. _____
3. _____

Today's affirmations :
_____
_____
_____

My mood today is...

- ○ Calm
- ○ Happy
- ○ Anxious
- ○ Rested
- ○ Angry
- ○ Playful
- ○ Creative
- ○ Sad
- ○ _____

Notes

> "In the multitude of my anxieties within me, Your comforts bring joy to my soul."
> Psalm 94:19

Checking - in

How are you *feeling* today? _____

Things you are *grateful* for :
1. _____
_____
2. _____
_____
3. _____
_____

Today's affirmations :
_____
_____
_____

My mood today is...

- ○ Calm
- ○ Rested
- ○ Creative

- ○ Happy
- ○ Angry
- ○ Sad

- ○ Anxious
- ○ Playful
- ○ _____

Notes

"In the multitude of my anxieties within me, Your comforts bring joy to my soul."
Psalm 94:19

Prayer for

1 Timothy 2:1-4

"I urge, then, first of all, that petitions, prayers, intercession and thanksgiving be made for all people—for kings and all those in authority, that we may live peaceful and quiet lives in all godliness and holiness".

example:
profession
home /family
school
church
jail
community
patients
students
leaders

Prayer for

1 Timothy 2:1-4

"I urge, then, first of all, that petitions, prayers, intercession and thanksgiving be made for all people—for kings and all those in authority, that we may live peaceful and quiet lives in all godliness and holiness".

example:
profession
home /family
school
church
jail
community
patients
students
leaders

Prayer for

1 Timothy 2:1-4

"I urge, then, first of all, that petitions, prayers, intercession and thanksgiving be made for all people—for kings and all those in authority, that we may live peaceful and quiet lives in all godliness and holiness".

example:
profession
home /family
school
church
jail
community
patients
students
leaders

Prayer for

1 Timothy 2:1-4

"I urge, then, first of all, that petitions, prayers, intercession and thanksgiving be made for all people—for kings and all those in authority, that we may live peaceful and quiet lives in all godliness and holiness".

example:
profession
home /family
school
church
jail
community
patients
students
leaders

Prayer for

1 Timothy 2:1-4

"I urge, then, first of all, that petitions, prayers, intercession and thanksgiving be made for all people—for kings and all those in authority, that we may live peaceful and quiet lives in all godliness and holiness".

example:
profession
home /family
school
church
jail
community
patients
students
leaders

www.ingramcontent.com/pod-product-compliance
Lightning Source LLC
Chambersburg PA
CBHW042358070526
44585CB00029B/2985